**PARENTS
-AND-
KIDS
SCIENCE**

24 ACTIVITIES FOR KIDS AND ADULTS TO SHARE

BY DANNY L. MCKENZIE

FEARON TEACHER AIDS

Executive Editor: Jeri Cipriano
Editor: Susan Eddy

Fearon Teacher Aids
An Imprint of Modern Curriculum
A Division of Simon & Schuster
299 Jefferson Road, P.O. Box 480
Parsippany, New Jersey 07054-0480

ISBN 0-86653-865-8

1 2 3 4 5 6 7 8 9   MAL   01 00 99 98 97 96

CONTENTS

INTRODUCTION

Why PAKS?

PAKS: *Parents-and-Kids Science* provides teachers with ready-to-use materials designed to get parents and children excited about science, to help establish a home-school connection, and to provide interesting learning activities for children to share with adults who are important in their lives. National parent surveys echo what we as professionals already know—that when parents, communities, and schools all work together, the result is a superior education for our country's children.

What Does PAKS Accomplish?

PAKS gets parents involved in developing their children's science process skills through 24 activities. Four activities each focus on the six skills of observation, inference, classification, communication, measurement, and prediction. Each activity invites children and parents to collect and record data.

Activities are not sequential and may be arranged in the order that best matches your curriculum. Materials needed to complete the activities are safe and readily available, and most can be provided by parents. Some materials, such as hand lenses and magnets, may need to be supplied by the school. All will fit easily into a one-gallon plastic zipper bag along with the activity and data recording sheets.

What Are the PAKS Components?

In addition to an activity sheet and data recording sheet for each of the 24 activities, **PAKS** includes a letter to parents (see page 10). The letter may be used as is or modified to suit your needs and should be sent home early in the year—before the first **PAKS** activity is sent. Six parent information sheets provide an overview of each process skill to assist parents in completing the activities with their children and to help them understand the importance of science in their children's lives. Send home the appropriate parent information sheet each time children begin work in a new skill area. You may wish to award a certificate to students who have completed the activities.

What Are **PAKS** Skills?

PAKS activities focus on six important science process skills. Often during science investigations, these skills are so integrated that they are no longer independently recognizable. **PAKS** activities help children develop these skills individually. Children are then able to integrate the skills as they move toward becoming competent investigators.

1. **OBSERVATION: perceiving objects and events, their properties, and their behaviors through the five senses.**

   Children learn about their world through their five senses: sight, sound, taste, smell, and touch. Common objects such as fruit, shells, and toys may be used to develop children's observational skills. For example, children might observe that apples are green on the outside, are juicy, make crunching noises when eaten, and are bigger than their mouths.

   Most observations made by children are *qualitative* in nature. For example, "the apple is yellow" or "the inside is white and mushy." However, qualitative observations may vary greatly among observers. One person may say an apple is yellow while another describes the same apple as golden. On the other hand, *quantitative* observations such as those including numbers and comparisons use standard units of measurement and are more precise. If a child observes that an apple has one stem and six seeds, it is likely that others observing the same apple would make the same quantitative observation. Both types of observations are useful and valuable.

   Children typically use the sense of sight more than the other senses and may need to be encouraged to use their senses of touch, smell, and hearing. The **PAKS** observation activities involve such common objects as rocks, salt, and leaves. Children will also observe how shadows change and how seltzer tablets dissolve in water of different temperatures.

2. **INFERENCE: a statement based on observation that attempts to explain or interpret the observed object or event.**

While sharing observations about apples, one child may say, "A bird tried to eat my apple." The child may think he or she is making an observation when, in fact, it is actually an inference—an attempt to explain the presence of a small hole in the apple. Other plausible inferences regarding the presence of a hole might include, "It fell from the tree and hit a rock" or "A branch poked a hole in it."

Inferences are attempts at explaining observations. They reflect the observers' past experiences and are not necessarily verifiable. As children make more observations about objects or events, their inferences may change. It is important for children to understand the difference between observations and inferences. In completing **PAKS** inference activities, children will make inferences about a "mystery object" sealed in a film canister, how sound is made, and which animals have nibbled on certain plants.

3. **CLASSIFICATION: grouping objects or events into categories based on specific characteristics or attributes.**

Given the tremendous number of objects and events in the world, it is neither possible nor desirable for children to study each one individually. By grouping objects and events, diversity becomes manageable and relationships become clear. Children may study characteristics and attributes of groups; look for similarities, differences, and patterns; and make generalizations that will serve as bases of concept development.

The simplest form of classification is often referred to as *binary*. In a binary system, objects are separated into two subsets based on one given characteristic. For example, forming two lines—boys in one line and girls in the other—is binary classification based on gender. You could separate the children into two groups based on other characteristics as well, such as hair color or types of shoes.

Almost any set of objects can be used for practice in binary classification. Children will work with seeds, leaves, and magnets in **PAKS** classification activities.

A more advanced type of classification is *multi-stage* classification—a succession of binary classifications. An example is to divide students into two subsets based on one characteristic, such as gender. The resulting subsets are then divided based on other characteristics, such as eye or hair color (see below). Typically, children need practice with simple binary classification before they can be successful with multi-stage classification.

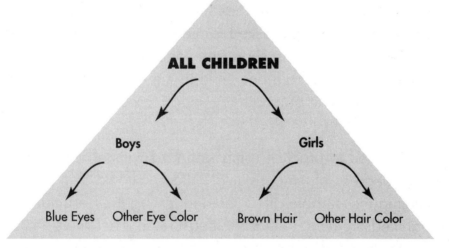

4. **COMMUNICATION: the transfer of information from one person to another by verbal, nonverbal, and/or written means.**

Communication in its many forms is basic to our interactions and relationships. Forms of communication that are particularly important in science include maps, charts, graphs, and drawings as well as the written and spoken word. All **PAKS** activities provide opportunities for children to practice communication. The four activities that focus specifically on communication involve children in graphing, charting, and using a checklist.

5. MEASUREMENT: a description of an object or event using numbers.

It is important for children to develop number sense as well as an understanding of the usefulness of measurement. When children make measurements, they are making quantitative observations. Before they can understand measurement as a process, however, children must know which attributes are measurable. Measurable attributes include *length, area, volume, weight, temperature,* and *time.*

Once children practice measurement in an activity using non-standardized units, they will see the need for standardization. For example, if children are asked to measure the length of a table using their pencils (some short and some long), they will discover that the results vary from one child to the next. It becomes evident that a standard unit of length is needed to communicate precisely the table's length.

Children need to practice using standard units of measurement such as degrees of temperature. Children should also practice estimating measurable attributes and testing their estimates through actual measurement. In **PAKS** measurement activities, children use both standard and nonstandard units of measurement.

6. PREDICTION: a forecast of what will happen based on previous observations.

Children make predictions every day. When they enter the classroom and see paint and paintbrushes on the table, they may predict that they will be painting. If they see papier mâché materials and fabric, they might predict they are going to make puppets. Children are able to make these predictions based on past experiences with art supplies. They have formulated models concerning the use of these materials in the classroom.

Predictions are based on models and models are based on experience. A guess is a forecast or prediction *not* based on experience. Experience is, therefore, extremely important to the development of future models and should be a primary consideration during prediction activities.

Opportunities to practice prediction occur often in school. When reading stories, you may ask children to predict what will happen next. In physical education activities such as tossing and catching bean bags, children learn to predict the amount of force it takes to throw objects and hit targets. During science activities, children may observe events and make predictions about the outcomes. In the **PAKS** prediction activities, children will observe and make predictions about mold on bread, seeds sprouting, and whether selected objects will sink or float.

Although each **PAKS** activity emphasizes a single skill, children will be practicing other science process skills at the same time. For example, when making predictions about mold growth, children will also be observing, measuring, and communicating. This integration of science process skills reflects the true nature of scientific investigation and will help start children on a rewarding path of curiosity, experimentation, and discovery.

Dear Parents:

This year, we will be using Parents-and-Kids Science (**PAKS**) activities as part of your child's science studies. **PAKS** activities are designed for children and adults to complete together at home. By sharing these activities with your children in a relaxed, comfortable environment, you will help foster an understanding and appreciation of science.

Children will bring home **PAKS** information sheets, activity sheets, and data recording sheets, along with most of the materials needed to complete the activities. Occasionally it may be necessary for you to supply household items, such as salt or vinegar.

The information and activity sheets will contain all the information you need. Activities should not take more than twenty minutes and may be completed at your convenience. As your child works, you may be expected to help by recording your child's answers, by asking specific "thinking" questions, or by assisting with materials. Don't be too concerned with right or wrong answers. Rather, invite your child to explore and investigate. Above all, the science time you share should be fun!

Your child will enjoy and benefit from the science time you share. Please feel free to contact me at any time regarding **PAKS** activities. I'd be most interested in your feedback.

Sincerely,

OBSERVATION

Examining Objects and Events Using Our Five Senses

Children learn about the world around them through their five senses: sight, taste, smell, touch, and hearing. Common objects, such as fruit and shells, may be used to develop children's observational skills. For example, children might observe that an apple is green on the outside, is juicy, makes a crunchy noise when bitten, feels firm and smooth, and is bigger than their mouths. Both adults and children tend to use their sense of sight more than their other senses. Therefore, your child may need some encouragement to use his or her senses of touch, smell, and hearing.

The skill of observation is important in science. Scientists spend much of their time making observations that help explain our world. The information children gather through their five senses leads to curiosity, questioning, thinking, and the creation of a knowledge base about their own environment. Observation is the basic science process skill that enables children to develop other skills, such as the ability to sort, classify, and make predictions.

Remember to have fun as you complete the **PAKS** observation activities.

NOW YOU SEE IT!

GOAL: To observe objects with a hand lens.

MATERIALS:
- Hand lens (magnifying glass)
- Objects to observe

PROCEDURE:
1. Gather several objects for your child to observe. Interesting things to look at might include salt, flower petals, leaves, wood, watches, jewelry, or rocks.

2. Ask your child to observe each object twice—first without the hand lens and then with the hand lens.

3. Encourage your child to draw what he or she sees on the Now You See It! Data Sheet.

FYI...

Light rays may change direction, or bend, as they travel through different materials. Both the hand lens and a water droplet cause light rays to move apart, thus producing a larger image that makes an object appear closer to the eye.

QUESTIONS TO ASK:
- How does the object look without the hand lens?
- What can you learn by using a hand lens?
- Are there other ways to make things look bigger? What are they?
- Can you find any lenses around the house?
- What else would you like to examine with a hand lens?

ADDITIONAL INVESTIGATIONS:
- Place a little water in a clear glass. Tip the glass toward you and look through the water at the print on this page. How does it look? (Print will appear larger and somewhat distorted.)
- Lay a piece of clear plastic wrap over this page. Place a large drop of water on the plastic wrap. Look at the print through the water drop from above and from the side. What appears to be happening? (Print will appear to rise from the paper.)
- Fill a glass half full of water. Place a pencil in the glass. How does the pencil look in the water? How does it appear to change as it enters the water? (Pencil will appear broken or bent at the point of entry.)

Now You See It!
DATA SHEET

Draw each object you observe
as it appears through the hand lens.

BUBBLE BUBBLE

GOAL: To observe what happens when seltzer tablets are placed in cold and hot water.

MATERIALS:
- 2 small clear plastic cups
- 2 seltzer tablets

FYI...

When the seltzer tablet is placed in water, a reaction occurs that gives off gas bubbles. When warm water is used, heat energy causes the reaction to occur at a faster rate.

PROCEDURE:

1. Prepare cold water by placing several ice cubes in one cup of water.

2. Pour cold water into a plastic cup and have your child draw the cup and water in the space labeled *A* on the Bubble Bubble Data Sheet.

3. Drop a seltzer tablet in the cold water and watch what happens.

4. Invite your child to draw what happened in the space labeled *B* on the data sheet.

5. Record your child's observations about the investigation on the back of the data sheet.

6. Repeat steps 2–5 using one cup of hot tap water instead of cold water. Have your child make "before and after" drawings in the spaces labeled *C* and *D* and record his or her observations.

QUESTIONS TO ASK:
- What happened when we dropped the first tablet in the cold water?
- Where do you think the bubbles went?
- What was the difference when we used hot instead of cold water? (Action of bubbles is louder and faster.)
- Describe any odor you noticed. (You may notice a medicinal smell.)

ADDITIONAL INVESTIGATIONS:
- Try dissolving seltzer tablets in other liquids, such as soft drinks, vinegar, or fruit juice.
- Place a tablet in a plastic zipper bag, add a small amount of water, seal the bag, and watch what happens.
- See how long it takes to dissolve tablets in water of varying temperatures.

NAME _____

BUBBLE BUBBLE
DATA SHEET

	Cold Water	Hot Water
BEFORE	A	C
AFTER	B	D

15

ME AND MY SHADOW

GOAL: To observe and describe shadows and think about why they change.

MATERIALS:
- chalk (if done on a sidewalk or driveway)
- pointed stick (if working on gravel)

PROCEDURE:
1. On a sunny morning, take your child to a flat area, such as a driveway, basketball court, or any level area that receives sunlight the entire day.
2. Trace around your child's shadow using chalk or a stick.
3. Have your child draw his or her shadow as it appears in your tracing in box 1 of the Me and My Shadow Data Sheet.
4. Be sure your child places his or her feet in the same location each time you trace the shadow. Repeat the above steps every two hours for a total of four drawings. Encourage your child to draw the resulting shadows in boxes 2–4.

QUESTIONS TO ASK:
- Which shadow was the longest?
- Which shadow was the shortest?
- How did your shadow change?
- Why do you think your shadow changed?

ADDITIONAL INVESTIGATIONS:
- Repeat this activity at different times of the year.
- Make shadows indoors using electric light and a variety of objects.
- Investigate how to make shadows change size.
- Go outside on a moonlit night and make moon shadows.

> **FYI...**
> As the earth rotates, the sun appears to move from east to west. In the early morning, the sun is low in the eastern sky and shadows are long and point toward the west. At midday, shadows are short and point north. In the afternoon, the sun is low in the western sky and shadows are once again long, but point east.

NAME _____

ME AND MY SHADOW
DATA SHEET

Draw the way your shadow looks at four different times.

Shadow 1	Shadow 2

Shadow 3	Shadow 4

 # NATURE HUNT

GOAL: To observe objects in nature.

MATERIALS:
- Crayons or colored markers

PROCEDURE:
1. This activity is a fun scavenger hunt. Take your child outdoors and find things that fit the description in each box of the Nature Hunt Data Sheet.

2. Encourage your child to examine closely each object and to use the senses of sight, touch, hearing, and smell to make some observations.

3. Share your own observations with your child.

QUESTIONS TO ASK:
- What does it look like?
- How does it feel?
- Does it make a sound? Describe it.
- Does it have an odor? Describe it.

ADDITIONAL INVESTIGATIONS:
- Create your own scavenger hunt inside your house or in a different outdoor location.
- Take a nature walk at a local state or national park, zoo, or botanical garden.

FYI...

The world is full of sounds, shapes, colors, odors, and textures. Children are experts at finding simple treasures to enjoy and share with adults. Try to see your child's miraculous world through his or her eyes.

NATURE HUNT
DATA SHEET

**Find one object that fits the description in each box.
Draw and color it.**

Something colorful	**Something that has an odor**
Something rough	**Something that makes a noise**

INFERENCE

Explaining What We Observe

When we attempt to explain an observation, we are making an *inference*. For example, children might explain the presence of a small hole in an apple (an observation) in different ways: "An insect ate part of the apple" or "a bird pecked the hole with his beak." Each statement is a possible explanation for the presence of the hole. Children base their inferences on prior experiences. For example, perhaps the child who stated that a bird made the hole has seen woodpeckers making holes in trees.

As children make more observations, their inferences may change. This reflects the nature of a true scientist. As scientists gather more and more data, their theories often change. This evolution of theories is one of the most exciting and interesting aspects of science.

SHAKE, RATTLE, AND ROLL

GOAL: To make inferences about what is inside a film canister.

MATERIALS:
- Black plastic film canister
- Objects and materials that will fit into the film canister, such as marbles, sand, rice, water, beans, salt (keep objects secret)

FYI...

During science investigations, children often make observations that lead to inferences. For example, a child may observe that a plant is wilted and infer that the plant needs water. Of course, a plant may also wilt if it receives too much water. Our inferences are not always correct!

PROCEDURE:
1. Place one of the objects into the canister and replace the top.
2. Challenge your child to guess what is inside the canister by shaking, rattling, and rolling the canister.
3. Record your child's observations on the Shake, Rattle, and Roll Data Sheet. After making several observations, your child may be able to guess (infer) what is in the canister.
4. Record your child's guess or have him or her draw what might be in the canister. Invite your child to open the canister and look inside.
5. Talk about your child's observations and guesses and compare them to observations of the actual object. It does not matter whether or not the guess is correct.
6. Repeat the activity at least two more times using other objects.

QUESTIONS TO ASK:
- Describe what you hear.
- What can you feel?
- How does the canister roll?
- What do you think is in the canister? What made you think so?

ADDITIONAL INVESTIGATIONS:
- Invite your child to put objects into the canister for you to infer what's inside.
- Make another inference box by placing larger mystery objects in a shoe box.

NAME _____

Shake, Rattle, and Roll
Data Sheet

My Observations   **My Guesses**

1. _____   1. _____

   _____   _____

2. _____   2. _____

   _____   _____

3. _____   3. _____

   _____   _____

4. _____   4. _____

   _____   _____

Do, Re, Mi

GOAL: To make inferences about sound.

MATERIALS:
- Three identical jars or drinking glasses
- Water
- Spoon

FYI...

When you tap the side of the glass, the glass vibrates. These vibrations travel to your ear and you "hear" them as sound. The more water there is in the glass, the slower the vibrations will be and the lower the pitch of the sound.

PROCEDURE:

1. Have your child fill one of the jars or glasses half-full of water and *gently* tap the side of the glass with the spoon.

2. Have your child fill another glass about 3/4 full and tap with the spoon. Ask if your child notices any difference in the two sounds.

3. Repeat the activity once more with a glass that is 1/4 full of water. Your child should observe that the more water there is in the glass, the lower the pitch.

4. Encourage your child to arrange the glasses from lowest to highest pitch and draw them on the Do, Re, Mi Data Table.

5. Ask your child to explain why the sound changes. He or she may say that the amount of water in a glass causes the sound to be different or that the amount of air causes the sound to change. Either inference is acceptable for young children.

QUESTIONS TO ASK:
- What did you hear when you tapped the glasses?
- What happened when you put more water in the glasses?
- Which glass makes a low sound? Which glass makes a high sound?
- Which glass has the most water? Which has the most air?

ADDITIONAL INVESTIGATIONS:
- Use additional glasses to make a musical scale and try playing simple tunes.
- Repeat the activity using soft drink bottles. Make sounds by blowing across the mouths of the bottles.

Do, Re, Mi
Data Sheet

Draw the glasses.

Low Sound	Middle Sound	High Sound

AIR BAG

GOAL: To make the inference that air can support weight.

MATERIALS:
- Plastic zipper bag
- Book

PROCEDURE:

1. Show your child the empty plastic zipper bag and ask if there is anything inside it. Invite your child to draw a picture of the empty bag on the Air Bag Data Sheet in the space labeled *Bag without Air*.

2. Help your child blow up the zipper bag and seal as much air as possible inside. Ask what is now inside the bag. Have your child draw the bag in the space labeled *Bag with Air*.

3. Encourage your child to predict what will happen when a book is placed on top of the inflated bag.

4. Invite your child to place a light book on top of the bag and observe what happens. Have him or her draw the bag and book in the space labeled *Bag with Air and Book*.

5. Help your child answer the question, "What is holding up the book?"

> ## FYI...
> Children often do not think of air as something that takes up space. They will say that a glass is empty unless it contains a visible substance. Your child may say that the plastic bag is empty even after it is filled with air. When the book is placed atop the bag and its weight is supported, your child will begin to understand that air inside the bag provides the support.

QUESTIONS TO ASK:
- How do you know there is air in the bag?
- How is a plastic bag like a basketball or football?
- What might happen if we put another book on top of the bag?

ADDITIONAL INVESTIGATIONS:
- Add additional books to see how much weight the inflated bag can support. Invite your child to make predictions first.
- Inflate a plastic trash bag and encourage your child to see if the bag will support his or her weight.
- Help your child find other examples of how air supports weight, such as automobile tires and inflatable rafts.

AIR BAG
DATA SHEET

Bag without Air

Bag with Air

Bag with Air and Book

What is holding up the book? _____

WHO EATS HERE?

GOAL: To make inferences about the kinds of animals that eat plants.

MATERIALS:
- Leaves, acorns, pine cones, flowers, and wood showing evidence of having been eaten or nibbled at by an animal (search for these with your child)

FYI...

Help your child understand that his or her inferences (kinds of animals) are based on observations (teeth marks on acorn or small holes in wood). If we do not make good observations, we probably will not make good inferences. Prior experiences are also important. Children who have watched animals eat will have less difficulty. Don't hesitate to assist your child if necessary.

PROCEDURE:
1. Invite your child to select two items from your collection to draw on the Who Eats Here? Data Sheet.
2. Ask your child to tell you what kind of animal might have nibbled on the items he or she drew. Have your child record these inferences on the data sheet.
3. Encourage your child to tell you why he or she thinks a particular animal made the marks or holes. Record the information on the data sheet under *Why?*

QUESTIONS TO ASK:
- See the Who Eats Here? Data Sheet

ADDITIONAL INVESTIGATIONS:
- Observe the behavior of pets (dogs, cats, mice, fish, birds) and make inferences about why animals act as they do.
- Look for animal tracks and infer what type of animal made the tracks. As your child makes inferences, encourage him or her to think about what information is being used to make these inferences.

NAME _____

WHO EATS HERE?
DATA SHEET

Who ate here?_____   Who ate here?_____

_____   _____

_____   _____

Why? _____   Why? _____

_____   _____

_____   _____

CLASSIFICATION

Grouping of Objects or Events

Classification is the process of grouping objects or events based on observable characteristics. Children learn to classify at an early age. They may classify foods (those they like and those that they don't) and toys (their toys and someone else's toys).

The simplest form of classification involves separating a group of objects into two sub-groups. For example, plants can be divided into two groups based on whether or not they have leaves. Animals can be divided based on whether or not they have backbones. However, plants and animals can be grouped in many other ways as well. Plants can be sorted according to whether or not they produce flowers. Animals can be divided between those that can fly and those that cannot. By studying group characteristics, children begin to develop a sense of the order of their world. This is important for future science studies.

SORTING SEEDS

GOAL: To classify seeds according to their characteristics.

MATERIALS:
- Seeds (bird seed or a collection of dried beans)
- Hand lens (optional)
- Glue

FYI...

Seeds exist in great variety—from tiny flower seeds to large coconuts. Some are transported by floating through the air and others by attaching themselves to animals or people. Humans eat many seeds, including grains and nuts.

PROCEDURE:

1. Encourage your child to observe the seed collection and think about ways in which the seeds are alike and ways in which they differ.

2. Invite your child to sort the seeds into two groups using an observable characteristic such as size, color, or shape.

3. Discuss the way in which the seeds were sorted. Help your child understand that there are other ways in which the seeds could have been sorted.

4. Have your child recombine the seeds and reclassify them using another set of characteristics.

5. Invite your child to select his or her favorite sorting method. Help him or her glue the sorted seeds onto the Seed Collection Sheet.

QUESTIONS TO ASK:
- How did you decide how to sort the seeds?
- In what other ways might you have sorted the seeds?

ADDITIONAL INVESTIGATIONS:
- Tie a white cotton sock to a string and pull it through a field or park. Encourage your child to remove and examine the seeds that stick to the sock.
- Make Crunchy Seed Candy.

  1 cup sunflower seeds (shelled)
  1 cup honey
  1 cup peanut butter (made from seeds!)
  1 cup cocoa powder (also made from seeds)
  1 cup sesame seeds

  Mix the first four ingredients and form one-inch balls. Roll balls in sesame seeds spread on waxed paper. Chill to harden.

NAME _____

SORTING SEEDS
DATA SHEET

I sorted these seeds according to _____ .

DOES IT ATTRACT?

GOAL: To classify objects according to whether or not they are attracted to a magnet.

MATERIALS:
- Magnet
- Collection of magnetic and non-magnetic objects

FYI...
Most magnets are made of iron. The iron atoms in a magnet are lined up in such a way that they attract other iron-containing objects.

PROCEDURE:
1. Encourage your child to experiment with the materials you have collected and the magnet.
2. Ask your child to sort the objects into two groups—those that are attracted to the magnet and those that are not.
3. Have your child draw and label the objects attracted to the magnet on the Does It Attract? Data Sheet.
4. Invite your child to search your home for objects that are attracted to magnets.

QUESTIONS TO ASK:
- Which objects does the magnet attract?
- Which objects are not attracted to the magnet?
- Do you think the magnet can pick up any of the objects? Which ones?
- How does it feel when you pull an object away from the magnet?
- How are the objects the magnet attracts alike?
- How are the objects the magnet does not attract alike?

ADDITIONAL INVESTIGATIONS:
- Investigate whether the magnetic force will pass through materials such as paper, water, and your hand.
- Search your house for magnets used in toys and appliances.
- Predict and then see how many paper clips your magnet will pick up.

DOES IT ATTRACT?
DATA SHEET

The magnet attracted these objects.	The magnet *did not* attract these objects.

 LIVING AND NON-LIVING

GOAL: To classify organisms and objects as living or non-living.

MATERIALS:
- Pencils, crayons, or markers

PROCEDURE:

1. Explain to your child that the two of you will play a game in which you decide whether a group of things are living or non-living.

2. Begin by selecting a living organism such as a plant, pet, or insect. Ask your child if the organism is living or non-living.

3. Help your child understand that the organism is living. Have your child either draw or write the name of the organism on the Living and Non-Living Data Sheet.

4. Continue to select and categorize both living and non-living things. Encourage your child to tell you why he or she is classifying an item as living or non-living.

FYI...

Most children think of living things as those that can move, play, eat, and sleep. The concepts of living and non-living can be challenging for children. They may say the sun is alive because it moves and has a face. Help your child understand that although living things move, not all things that move are alive.

QUESTIONS TO ASK:
- Why do you think this item is living (or non-living)?
- How are all the living organisms you found the same?
- How do living organisms differ from non-living objects?

ADDITIONAL INVESTIGATIONS:
- Identify some non-living objects that have characteristics of living organisms. For example, toys that move and crystals that grow.
- Examine the life history of an organism such as an insect. Examine how it grows, moves, responds, and reproduces.
- Sprout bean seeds and watch them grow, move, and respond to light.

LIVING AND NON-LIVING
DATA SHEET

Living

Non-Living

SORTING LEAVES

GOAL: To classify leaves according to their characteristics.

MATERIALS:
- Leaves
- Crayons or markers

FYI...

Leaves come in many shapes, sizes, and colors. They may be oval, long, round, needle-like, or shaped like hands. Be sure not to collect any poisonous leaves such as poison sumac, poison oak, or poison ivy.

PROCEDURE:

1. Begin by collecting one leaf from four to six different species of trees. The types of trees are not important. Try to find leaves that differ in shape, size, color, or in other observable ways.

2. Ask your child to describe each leaf to you and encourage him or her to sort the leaves into two groups based on criteria of his or her choice.

3. Have your child draw each group in the space labeled *First Sort* on the Sorting Leaves Data Sheet.

4. Discuss your child's criteria for leaf sorting.

5. Put the leaves back into one group and have your child sort them again, using another characteristic.

6. Invite your child to draw the two new groups in the space labeled *Second Sort*.

7. Repeat the activity a third time.

QUESTIONS TO ASK:
- How did you sort the leaves?
- Are all the leaves alike? How?
- Are all the leaves different? How?
- How do leaves change?

ADDITIONAL INVESTIGATIONS:
- Sort other plant parts, such as flowers or fruits.
- Make leaf rubbings by placing leaves under pieces of paper and rubbing over them with the side of a crayon.

SORTING LEAVES
DATA SHEET

First Sort

Second Sort

Third Sort

COMMUNICATION

The Giving of Information from One Person to Another

Communication is one of the most important skills for children to practice. Humans communicate in many ways—through talking, drawing, writing, singing, dancing, and acting. Forms of communication that are especially important in science include maps, charts, graphs, and drawings. Of course, written and verbal communication are important as well.

Encourage children to be specific when communicating in science. For example, when observing a flower, you might count the number of petals, note the colors, describe the aroma, measure the width, record where you found the flower, and draw it. This communicates a much clearer picture of the flower than simply saying, "It's pretty!"

THE SKY'S THE LIMIT

GOAL: To communicate by making a weather chart.

MATERIALS:
- Markers or crayons

PROCEDURE:

1. Invite your child to observe the sky and weather each day for one week—at the same time each day, if possible. After each observation, discuss what your child has observed.

2. Encourage your child to draw and label these observations in the appropriate boxes on the Sky's the Limit Data Sheet. Children may use the symbols provided or create their own.

3. Be sure to discuss with your child how the weather changed (or stayed the same) during the week once the data sheet is complete.

FYI...

Weather is the condition of the air at a given time and place. A first step in weather forecasting is to observe current conditions. White, fluffy clouds (cumulus) are usually associated with fair or partly sunny weather. Feather-like clouds very high in the sky (cirrus) usually indicate cold weather and often mean that fair weather will change. Large, low, layered clouds (stratus) cover the sky and precede stormy, rainy, or snowy weather.

QUESTIONS TO ASK:
- How does the sky look today? How did it look yesterday?
- How does the sky look when it is raining? Snowing?
- Why is it important to know what the weather will be?

ADDITIONAL INVESTIGATIONS:
- Challenge your child to make weather observations for a period of one month.
- Examine newspaper weather maps and forecasts with your child.
- Watch local TV weather reports and record the high and low temperatures for each day on a chart.

The Sky's the Limit
Data Sheet

Sunday	Monday	Tuesday	Wednesday

Thursday	Friday	Saturday

Sunny

Sunny With Clouds

Cloudy

Rainy

Snow or Ice

TANTALIZING TANGRAMS

GOAL: To communicate information to another person.

MATERIALS:
- Tangrams
- Crayons or markers

> **FYI...**
> Tangrams are Chinese puzzles made by cutting a square into the seven shapes shown on the pattern page. These shapes can be recombined to make many different figures.

PROCEDURE:

1. Have your child color the tangrams as indicated.

2. Carefully cut out the tangrams for your child.

3. Help your child use all the tangram pieces to form a square. As you are doing this, describe or have your child describe each action. For example, "Place the large blue triangle beside the large red triangle" or "Place the small blue triangle in the corner."

4. Have your child reassemble the tangrams into other shapes. Encourage your child to describe what he or she is doing.

5. Now invite your child to give you directions to make a shape or pattern using all the tangrams. If your child's directions are not clear, demonstrate why they are difficult to follow before helping to clarify the directions.

6. Finally, invite your child to follow *your* directions to make a shape or pattern.

QUESTIONS TO ASK:
- Where or when do you need to follow instructions?
- How can you be sure someone understands your directions?
- How can you be a good listener?
- What can you do if instructions are unclear?

ADDITIONAL INVESTIGATIONS:
- Allow your child to prepare simple foods (such as instant pudding or flavored drink mix) as you read the directions aloud. Talk about what could happen if the directions were out of order.
- Have your child tell you the steps needed to complete a simple task such as washing dishes, packing for a trip, or playing a game.

TANGRAM PATTERNS

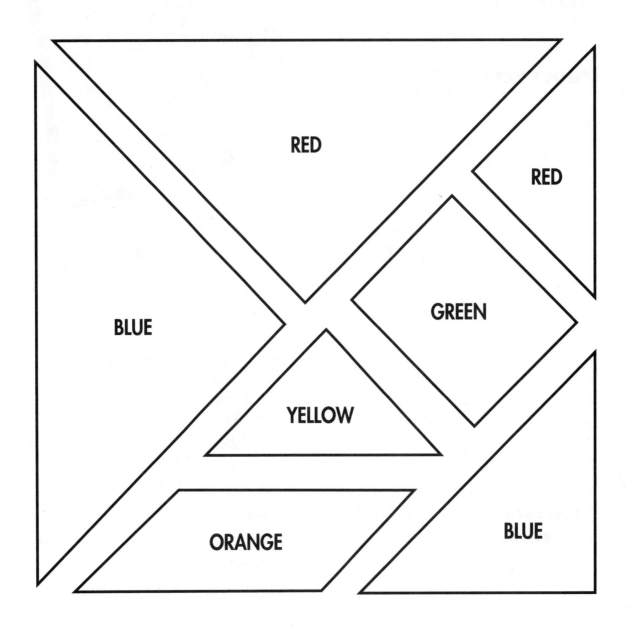

RED

RED

BLUE

GREEN

YELLOW

ORANGE

BLUE

PICTOGRAPH

GOAL: To communicate information by making a pictograph.

MATERIALS:
- 12 pairs of socks
- Pictograph chart
- Pencil
- Crayons

FYI...

Graphing is an important communications skill. The pictograph is a simple type of graph that uses pictures to represent objects. After learning to make pictographs, children can move on to making bar graphs.

PROCEDURE:

1. Invite your child to group the 24 socks by color and count the number of socks in each color group.

2. Have your child record the number of socks in each color group on the Pictograph Data Sheet. For example, if three pairs of socks are red, your child should draw and color a pair of socks in boxes 1, 2, and 3 in the column labeled *red*.

3. If a group of socks do not fit into one of the labeled categories (white, black, blue, green, red, or brown) help your child label the blank column appropriately (pink, striped, gray).

4. After completing the pictograph, encourage your child to share the findings with another family member.

QUESTIONS TO ASK:
- How many pairs of white socks do we have? (Repeat for other color groups.)
- What does our pictograph show?
- What do the numbers on the pictograph mean?
- How many socks do we have altogether?

ADDITIONAL INVESTIGATIONS:
- Encourage your child to make pictographs showing the make-up of other groups of objects such as building blocks, shoes, books, crayons, cars, or coins.

PICTOGRAPH
DATA SHEET

🧦 = 1 Pair of Socks

	White	Black	Blue	Green	Red	Brown
10						
9						
8						
7						
6						
5						
4						
3						
2						
1						

COLOR OF SOCKS

ANIMAL CHECKLIST

GOAL: To communicate information by using a checklist.

MATERIALS:
- Pencil
- Animal to observe

PROCEDURE:

1. Explain to your child that you are going to fill out an Animal Checklist that will require observations and recording information.

2. Select an animal to observe. You may wish to observe a pet or you may prefer to go outdoors and observe an insect, bird, or other animal.

3. The questions on the Animal Checklist Data Sheet will guide your child's observations. Have your child place a check under the correct answer for each question.

4. After the data sheet is complete, write the name of the animal at the bottom of the page.

QUESTIONS TO ASK:
- See the Animal Checklist Data Sheet.

ADDITIONAL INVESTIGATIONS:
- Challenge another family member to guess the animal your child observed by looking at the completed checklist. (Be sure to cover the name of the animal at the bottom of the sheet.)
- Complete a checklist for a different animal. Compare and contrast the two checklists.

©1996 Fearon Teacher Aids

NAME _____

ANIMAL CHECKLIST
DATA SHEET

Does your animal have:	Yes	No
Hair or fur	_____	_____
Feathers	_____	_____
Scales	_____	_____
Wings	_____	_____
Legs	_____	_____
Fins	_____	_____

Does your animal:

Fly	_____	_____
Walk	_____	_____
Swim	_____	_____
Crawl	_____	_____
Make a sound	_____	_____

The animal is _____ _____

MEASUREMENT

Describing an Object or Event by Using Numbers

When children make measurements, they are simply making observations with numbers. Measurement is an important science skill—scientists spend a great deal of time making measurements. Various characteristics of objects may be measured, including weight, length, width, volume, and area. Measurement activities for young children should focus on counting and measuring length, width, time, and temperature.

Estimation is an important aspect of numbers and measurement. It is important to give children opportunities to estimate measurements such as temperature and length. They should then make the actual measurements to see how close their estimates are to the actual value.

PAPER CLIPPING

GOAL: To measure length using a paper clip.

MATERIALS:
- Paper clip
- Assorted objects to measure (crayon, pencil, piece of string, book, box)

FYI...

Children begin to learn about measurement by measuring in nonstandard units such as paper clips. We all use nonstandard units of measure (a pinch of salt) as well as standard measures such as feet, meters, grams, gallons, and miles.

PROCEDURE:
1. Explain that you will work together to measure several objects using the length of a paper clip as a unit of measurement.

2. Demonstrate by measuring the length of your longest finger using the paper clip. Round to the nearest whole paper clip. Depending on the size of the paper clip, your finger will measure two or three paper clips in length.

3. Invite your child to measure the length of his or her longest finger using the paper clip and record this measurement on the Paper Clipping Data Sheet.

4. Help your child measure each of the objects you have selected. Have your child record the measurements on the Paper Clipping Data Sheet.

QUESTIONS TO ASK:
- Why do we measure things?
- What are some things we could use to measure with besides a paper clip?
- What can be measured besides length?
- What does a car's speedometer measure? A measuring cup? A thermometer?

ADDITIONAL INVESTIGATIONS:
- Encourage your child to develop and use a nonstandard unit of measure such as a pencil, penny, or little finger.
- Challenge your child to measure all the objects again using a standard unit of measure (inches or centimeters).

PAPER CLIPPING
DATA SHEET

Object	Measurement in Paper Clips
My finger	

JUMPING JACKS

GOAL: To measure heart rate, time, and number of jumping jacks.

MATERIALS:
- Digital watch or watch with sweep second hand

PROCEDURE:

1. Determine your child's heart rate by placing two fingers on the child's wrist or on the side of his or her neck where you feel the pulse. Count the number of pulses in one minute.

2. Have your child record this resting pulse rate on the Jumping Jacks Data Sheet on the first line of the *Number of Heartbeats* column.

3. Invite your child to do ten jumping jacks and measure the heart rate again. Record the heart rate on the second line of the heartbeat column (opposite 10 jumping jacks).

4. After a five minute rest period, have your child do 20 jumping jacks. Record the heart rate.

5. Repeat the activity with 30 and 40 jumping jacks. Be sure to allow a five minute rest between trials.

QUESTIONS TO ASK:
- What happened to your heart rate when you did the jumping jacks?
- How did you feel after doing the jumping jacks?
- What are some things we measured in this experiment?
- How did we measure time? Heart rate? Number of jumping jacks?

ADDITIONAL INVESTIGATIONS:
- Repeat the activity using different exercises (running in place, dancing, playing a sport).
- Measure the time needed to run different distances.
- Have your child measure your heart rate while you perform the jumping jacks and record the statistics on the same data sheet. Compare your pulse rate with your child's.

JUMPING JACKS
DATA SHEET

Number of Jumping Jacks	Number of Heartbeats
0	_____
10	_____
20	_____
30	_____
40	_____

What happened when you exercised?

_____

_____

_____

WHAT'S THE METER?

GOAL: To measure objects using the metric system.

MATERIALS:
- Metric ruler

PROCEDURE:

1. Invite your child to examine the metric ruler. Have him or her show you the numbers on the ruler and explain to you why they are there.

2. Have your child measure the various objects listed on the What's the Meter Data Sheet and record the results. Watch closely to be sure the measurements are precise.

QUESTIONS TO ASK:
- Why are there numbers on the ruler?
- What do the numbers mean?
- Why is it important to be able to measure things?
- What are some other ways we measure things?

ADDITIONAL INVESTIGATIONS:
- Take your child shopping and identify ways you use measurement as you shop. For example, we use measurement when buying milk, soft drinks, gasoline, batteries, light bulbs, and clothes.
- Encourage your child to imagine a day without measurement. How would the day be different?

WHAT'S THE METER?
DATA SHEET

My pencil is _____ centimeters long.

This sheet of paper is _____ centimeters long.

This sheet of paper is _____ centimeters wide.

My thumb is _____ centimeters long.

My pointer finger is _____ centimeters long.

My nose is _____ centimeters long.

My foot is _____ centimeters long.

_____ is _____ centimeters long.

_____ is _____ centimeters long.

TAKING TEMPERATURES

GOAL: To measure and record temperatures using a thermometer.

MATERIALS:
- Indoor/outdoor thermometer
- Plastic cup
- Water
- Ice cube or two spoonfuls of crushed ice

FYI...

Your child may have difficulty reading the thermometer. With your assistance, he or she should understand that the numbers correspond to the amount of heat present. Do not allow children to take their own temperatures or place laboratory thermometers in their mouths. If you wish to take your child's temperature as part of this activity, use an approved oral thermometer.

PROCEDURE:

1. Examine the thermometer together and show your child how to read the current temperature.

2. Place the thermometer outdoors for approximately five minutes. Help your child read the temperature and record it on the Taking Temperatures Data Sheet.

3. Continue by taking temperatures inside your home, in your refrigerator, and the freezer.

4. Fill the plastic cup three-quarters full of tap water. Have your child place the thermometer in the water and measure and record the temperature.

5. Have your child add ice to the water. After five minutes, measure and record the water temperature.

6. Encourage your child to measure other temperatures such as bath water, milk, or rainwater and record the results on the data sheet.

QUESTIONS TO ASK:
- When was the temperature the hottest? The coldest?
- Why is it important to know the temperature outside?

ADDITIONAL INVESTIGATIONS:
- Measure the outside temperature at the same time each day for a week. Record the results on a data sheet.
- On a sunny day, place two thermometers outdoors, one under a black piece of paper, the other under a white piece of paper. Compare the temperatures.

Taking Temperatures
Data Sheet

Inside _____

Outside _____

Refrigerator _____

Freezer _____

Tap Water _____

Ice Water _____

_____

_____

_____

_____

PREDICTION

A Forecast of What Will Happen

Children make predictions every day. If they enter a classroom and see paint and paintbrushes, they may predict that they will be painting. This prediction would be based on past experiences with paint and paintbrushes. Adults make predictions as well. You may predict, for example, that your next gas or electric bill will be high because of the heat you used during very cold weather. This is also a prediction based upon past experience. A guess is a forecast that is *not* based on experience. It is usually not as accurate as a prediction. In science, children are encouraged to become good predictors. This can only be accomplished when children conduct scientific investigations.

MOLDY BREAD

GOAL: To predict how mold grows.

MATERIALS:
- Slice of bread
- 1 gallon plastic zipper bag
- Crayons

FYI...

As children make observations over time, they become better predictors of what will happen next. Hopefully, your child will be able to predict that the mold growth on the bread will increase and that color changes will occur.

PROCEDURES:

1. Have your child place the bread on the floor and press on it gently. Sprinkle a few drops of water on the side of the bread that made contact with the floor.

2. Help your child place the bread in the plastic bag and seal it tightly. Please do *not* open the bag at any time during the investigation. Some people may be allergic to the molds that will grow on the bread.

3. Ask your child how he or she thinks the bread will look in three days. Have your child draw that prediction in the box labeled *Day 3* on the Moldy Bread Data Sheet.

4. Put the plastic bag containing the bread in a warm, dark place such as a closet or drawer. After three days, have your child examine the piece of bread and draw it in the observation box labeled *Day 3*.

5. Invite your child to predict and draw how the bread will appear in another three days. On day six, have your child observe and draw the changes to the bread. Repeat the process for day nine.

QUESTIONS TO ASK:
- What do you see happening to the bread?
- Why do you think the bread is changing?
- How did your predictions compare with your observations?
- Can you think of other things that might change like the bread did? (For example, fruit.)

ADDITIONAL INVESTIGATIONS:
- Place an object such as a slice of apple, a rock, ice cube, leaf, or piece of candy in a jar and seal with a lid. Have your child predict how the object will change.

NAME _____

MOLDY BREAD
DATA SHEET

Prediction	Observation
Day 3	**Day 3**
Day 6	**Day 6**
Day 9	**Day 9**

BALL BOUNCE

GOAL: To predict how high a ball will bounce when dropped.

MATERIALS:
- Bouncing ball
- Measuring tape or 2-meter strip of paper marked in centimeters

FYI...
Children often use prediction skills when they play games. For example, when playing basketball, a child may predict how the ball will bounce off the backboard or where it will travel when bounced off the court.

PROCEDURE:
1. Tape the measuring tape to a wall or door. The end marked *zero* should just touch the floor.

2. Hold the ball against the measuring tape at a height of approximately 100 cm (36 inches). Ask your child to read the height and record it on the Ball Bounce Data Sheet in the box labeled *Height of Drop* under the heading *Drop 1*.

3. Ask your child how high the ball might bounce if you were to drop it. Have your child place a finger on the measuring tape at the predicted bounce height.

4. Record the predicted height of bounce in the box labeled *Predicted Height of Bounce*.

5. Drop the ball and watch closely to see how high it bounces. Record the height of bounce on the data table in the box labeled *Actual Height of Bounce*.

6. Repeat using four different drop heights. Be sure your child records a prediction before you drop the ball.

QUESTIONS TO ASK:
- What happened when the ball was dropped from the top of the tape measure? Why?
- What happened when the ball was dropped from near the bottom of the tape measure? Why? (Dropping the ball from a higher point gives the ball more energy which translates into a higher bounce.)

ADDITIONAL INVESTIGATIONS:
- Repeat the activity using different types of balls.
- Have your child predict the number of bounces when the ball is dropped from different heights.

BALL BOUNCE
DATA SHEET

DROP NUMBER

	1	2	3	4	5
Height of Drop					
Predicted Height of Bounce					
Actual Height of Bounce					

BEAN SPROUTS

GOAL: To predict how a bean will change as it sprouts.

MATERIALS:
- 2 beans, such as dry lima beans
- 2 clear plastic cups
- 2 paper towels
- Crayons or markers

FYI...

Your child may be challenged when asked to predict how the beans will change. If so, explain that beans are really just seeds that can grow into plants if they have water and sunlight.

PROCEDURE:

1. Invite your child to examine the beans.

2. Fold the paper towels and place them in the cups so that the bottoms and sides of the cups are covered.

3. Slide a bean between the paper towel and the side of each cup. The beans should be visible.

4. Slowly add water to *one* of the cups so that the paper towel and bean become moist. Label this cup *Wet.* Label the other cup *Dry.*

5. Have your child draw both beans in the boxes labeled *How the beans looked at the start* on the data sheet. *Remind your child to check the wet bean each day and add enough water to keep it moist.*

6. Have your child draw a prediction of how each bean will look in one week in the appropriate boxes on the data sheet.

7. After one week, have your child draw how the beans look in the appropriate boxes on the data sheet. Discuss the changes that have occurred. Compare the last drawings your child made with the predictions.

QUESTIONS TO ASK:
- Do you think the beans will change? How? Why?
- How did the beans change during the time you observed them?
- How do you think the beans will look after two weeks?

ADDITIONAL INVESTIGATIONS:
- Place the sprouted bean in a cup of soil and have your child continue to make observations and predictions.
- Place an Irish potato in a cup of water and have your child observe how the potato sprouts and grows.

BEAN SPROUTS
DATA SHEET

	Wet	Dry
How the beans looked at the start.		
How I think they will look in one week.		
How they looked in one week.		

SINK OR FLOAT?

GOAL: To predict if objects will sink or float when placed in water.

MATERIALS:
- Penny, dime, piece of wood, paper clip, ping-pong ball, rubber band, egg, rock (or objects of your choice)
- Bowl of water

FYI...

Sinking and floating are important concepts in elementary science. Children often think that things that are heavy will sink and things that are light will float. Whether an object floats or sinks is determined by its density (how closely the atoms in the object are packed together). A heavy object such as a boat will float. A light object such as a paper clip will sink. Sinking and floating investigations set the stage for children's later understanding of the concept of density.

PROCEDURE:
1. Invite your child to examine each object and predict whether it will sink or float in water. Encourage your child to give a reason for each prediction.
2. After recording the prediction on the data sheet in the column labeled *Predictions*, have your child place the object in the water to see if it sinks or floats.
3. Have your child record what actually happened in the column labeled *Observations*.

QUESTIONS TO ASK:
- Why do you think the object floats (or sinks)?
- What do all the objects that sink have in common?
- How are the floating objects different from those that sink?
- Do you know of any other objects that float?
- Can you think of any other objects that sink?

ADDITIONAL INVESTIGATIONS:
- Test additional objects to see if they will sink or float.
- Identify ways we use things that float, such as life preservers and fishing corks, and how we use things that sink, such as anchors and fishing weights.

SINK OR FLOAT?
DATA SHEET

	Predictions	Observations
Penny		
Dime		
Wood		
Paper clip		
Ping-pong ball		
Rubber band		
Egg		
Rock		